Original title:
The Mystery Beneath the Waves

Copyright © 2025 Creative Arts Management OÜ
All rights reserved.

Author: Maya Livingston
ISBN HARDBACK: 978-1-80587-354-9
ISBN PAPERBACK: 978-1-80587-824-7

Beneath the Shimmer

The fish wear crowns, quite absurd,
With jellybeans for their dessert.
Crabs do the cha-cha on the sand,
While octopuses lend a hand.

Sea turtles flaunt their funky styles,
Snapping selfies, wearing smiles.
Starfish debate whose arms are best,
In an undersea fashion contest!

Lost Lore of the Ocean

Clams gossip loud about their pearls,
Whales do ballet in giant swirls.
A narwhal jokes with a dolphin friend,
About the dingy seaweed trend.

Mermaids giggle, sharing tea,
With sea urchins drunk on glee.
Sharks in suits, they discuss their fate,
"Who needs snacks when you can debate?"

Depths of Wonder

The sea cucumber's a veggie prank,
Plants dance like it's a hip-hop rank.
A treasure chest full of silly socks,
Who knew deep blue had such fun clocks?

Anglerfish with their glowing lights,
Throw raves in the ocean nights.
Blowfish puff, trying to scare,
But they're just jokes, with bubbles to spare!

The Call of the Abyss

In the dark where shadows play,
Crustaceans plan their grand buffet.
Whimsical tales on the sea floor,
With a pirate who can't find the door.

Anemones dance a wobbly jig,
Seahorses ride a giant pig.
The depths are loud, full of cheer,
Join the party, swim down here!

Submerged Whispers

In the ocean's depths, fish wear chef hats,
Mollusks gossip spiced with chitchat.
Seaweed dances, twirls in delight,
While crabs moonwalk, it's quite the sight.

Eels play tag in a swirling game,
The starfish cheer, but can't make a name.
A whale sings karaoke so fine,
While dolphins jump, sipping brine.

Legends of the Liquid World

Tales of a sunken pirate ship,
Where fish tell jokes and dolphins quip.
Octopuses throw wild disco raves,
While sea urchins hide in colorful caves.

Anemones juggle, oh what a show,
While clownfish giggle in a row.
Mermaids laugh during their tea,
Caught in a whirlpool, it's quite the spree!

Rhythms of the Hidden Depths

Bubbles pop like confetti in the air,
Seahorses waltz without a care.
Sharks in tuxedos, looking quite slick,
Crack jokes at the reef—oh, what a trick!

The jellyfish flash like disco lights,
While turtles spin in their fancy flights.
A puffer fish inflates with pride,
Chasing a treasure chest, oh, what a ride!

Dreams Adrift

In dreams of tides, turtles take a cruise,
Building sandcastles, they don't snooze.
A seagull juggles shells with flair,
While a grouper hides in a comfy chair.

The sea foam whispers giggly tales,
About lost flippers and fishy trails.
Starfish play cards, oh, what a game,
Finding lost socks is their claim to fame!

The Siren's Call

Oh, listen close to the wavy tune,
Where fish wear hats and sing to the moon.
A mermaid's giggle floats on the sound,
While crabs do the Charleston, dancing around.

The fishermen shrug, their lines disappear,
As seahorses boast of their cavalier.
Pufferfish giggle, with cheeks puffed wide,
Making waves like laughter, in the tide.

Tidal Riddles

A sea turtle plays with a jellyfish ball,
Telling tales to the clams who can't help but sprawl.
The tide rolls in, but it's all a jest,
As dolphins juggle shells, they're quite the best.

Octopuses hide playing peek-a-boo,
With all of their arms, they're never quite through.
Whales crack jokes in their deep ocean halls,
While sea cucumbers roll in fits and falls.

Forgotten Shipwrecks

Down where the old ships rust, what a sight,
Skeletons dance, taking off into the night.
A parrotfish squawks, "This place is a hoot!"
As pirates play bingo with barnacle loot.

Treasure maps written in knock-knock jokes,
While starfish giggle at wise old folks.
Anchors are hanging like party streamers,
Full of fish jokes and far-fetched dreamers.

Chasing Phantoms

Ghost ships glide under the moon's bright eye,
With a crew of old socks that no longer fly.
They argue and bicker about their lost treasure,
As crabs hold a meeting, such a strange pleasure.

Eels dash around, like shadows in flight,
While octopuses tease, "Let's sneak up tonight!"
But their laughter echoes, it's all in good fun,
As they dodge jellybeans and a rogue flying bun.

Murmurs from Below

Bubbles giggle, fish all chatter,
Octopus is wearing a new hat.
Crabs are holding a dance-off now,
Seahorses judge with a raised brow.

A whale tells jokes, but they fall flat,
Jellyfish glow, but can't throw a mat.
Starfish snicker at turtle races,
And dolphins laugh in silly places.

Nautical Enigmas

Barnacles gossip on the ship's hull,
While a clam's stuck in nonsense with a dull lull.
Pufferfish puff not for show,
But to scare off a squid in tow.

Seashells spin tales of treasure chests,
But all they hold are old sea jest.
Mermaids swim with sparkly tails,
Trading fish stories filled with wails.

The Twilight Tide

At dusk, waves giggle and play hide and seek,
With crabs in costumes, oh how unique!
Squid's got the moves, with his eight limbs jive,
While plankton's disco keeps the beat alive.

The tides bring tales of a fish on a quest,
Chasing after seaweed, thinking it's best.
As the moon winks down with a silver glow,
The ocean's silliness starts to flow.

Forgotten Echoes of the Sea

A pirate's ghost lost his parrot, it seems,
Now he haunts the sea with ridiculous dreams.
The treasure he seeks is a sock, not gold,
While seagulls squawk stories long trolled.

Old shipwrecks chuckle with secrets untold,
As barnacles dance in the ocean so bold.
Echoes of laughter resound and surprise,
In the underwater world, where humor lies.

Sunken Truths

Where fish wear hats and dance all night,
Octopuses swap tales with delight.
Mermaids giggle, flipping their hair,
As dolphins hold court in the salty air.

A sunken ship with a treasure chest,
Full of socks, it caused quite a jest.
Seagulls squawk, what a strange find!
Who knew the ocean was so unrefined!

Sea cucumbers play the people's foe,
Tickling toes of folks on boats that row.
Behind a coral, a crab now grins,
Poking fun at the fish who can't swim thin.

Sardines sing songs, a catchy tune,
While turtles race under a big balloon.
Though the sea's deep, it's full of cheer,
Join the fun, just don't get too near!

Fathoms of Silence

In depths where silence rules the day,
A clam tells jokes in a clever way.
Jellyfish glow with laughter so bright,
While anglerfish show off their light!

A cricket chirps in an old sea shell,
Sings of adventures, oh what a swell!
Anemones giggle, tickled with glee,
As starfish tease—their hands are so free!

In the trenches, a whale's hearty laugh,
Echoes through waves as it takes a bath.
While schools of tiny fish trade glances,
Creating splashes and playful chances.

Cautious squids in slick attire,
Play hide-and-seek, oh, they never tire.
With each new wave, the fun won't cease,
In the hush of the ocean, there's always peace!

Hidden Voices of the Deep

Bubbles pop like jokes in the night,
As sea horses dance in dazzling light.
A whale hums a tune, so wacky and grand,
Making neighbors shift in the sandy land.

Little shrimp host a crazy parade,
In costumes made of seaweed, hand-made.
A crab runs for office, "Vote for me!"
But all he does is dance and flee!

Grouper fish gossip, they chat and munch,
While sea urchins sit alone for lunch.
A starfish criticizes their chatter,
But laughs out loud—what's the matter!

In the abyss, the laughter swells,
With floppy eels casting their spells.
The ocean's a stage for a comical show,
Where every little creature puts on a glow!

Abyssal Secrets

An ancient wreck with a hat for a crown,
The captain's snoring can be heard all around.
His pet eel practicing stand-up, it's true,
With punchlines that make even sharks turn blue!

Crabs are rehearsing their latest play,
In a grassy patch where they love to sway.
Seahorses critiquing the plot's weak twist,
And jellyfish are all on the guest list!

A porpoise juggles some colorful shells,
While seaweed sways and at laughing yells.
An old octopus drags a mic to the show,
Sings of the treasures that we'll never know!

Down in the deep where secrets abound,
The antics of fish just seem to astound.
With each little splash, we share a good cheer,
In the depths of the sea, there's nothing to fear!

Beneath the Glimmering Surface

Bubbles laugh as fish do swim,
With silly grins and fins so slim.
A crab makes jokes, a clown in shell,
Telling tales of the sea's odd spell.

The octopus winks with eight arms wide,
As seaweed dances, placing a guide.
A dolphin squeaks, 'Where's the party?'
Fish in tuxedos, feeling quite hearty.

The seahorse gallops, what a sight,
With tiny top hats, ready for night.
They tango and cha-cha, a splashy dance,
In a world where nonsense takes a chance.

From coral castles to sandy floors,
Laughter echoes, a sound that soars.
Amidst the waves, joy resonates,
Where the fun and folly never waits.

Drowned Melodies

Old barnacles hum a jaunty tune,
While starfish strum with a fork and spoon.
A whale sings bass, a jellyfish jives,
Grooving to sounds of aquatic lives.

The sea turtles are tapping their feet,
In bubbles of rhythm, they can't be beat.
A conch shell shouts, 'Turn up the bass!'
We dance under sea foam, a colorful place.

Eels play slinkies, oh what a sight,
As sea otters juggle, what a delight!
Clams become drums, making beats so fine,
In this underwater concert, we intertwine.

From fishy choirs to shellfish bands,
Everyone's jamming, no strict commands.
So here in the deeps, we all agree,
Life's a party, just wait and see!

Shadows of the Deep Sea

In the murk where shadows prance,
Squid tap dance, in deep sea pants.
A lurking shark is quite the tease,
With goofy grins, oh, if you please.

Deep down low, where lanterns glow,
The angler's light gets quite the show.
A fish with a mustache starts to croon,
To all the critters 'neath the moon.

Phantom figures glide by with flair,
While a clownfish jokes, 'Is it Halloween air?'
With ghostly whispers from the frightful swell,
We scatter laughter, a bubbling spell.

A treasure chest filled not with gold,
But rubber ducks and toys of old.
In shadows deep, it's quite a scene,
Where giggles echo, from unseen to seen.

The Silent Depth

In the silent depths where ripples play,
A fish with a top hat winks today.
With sea cucumber pals, so bizarre,
They spin and twirl, a dancing bazaar.

Quietly lurking, a clam's big grin,
With shells that spin and tales to spin.
They whisper secrets soft as sea foam,
In this wacky underwater home.

A turtle whispers, 'Keep it hushed!'
While sipping seaweed in a lush brushed.
The deep is quiet, yet brightly loud,
With hidden antics, this place is proud.

So dive into silence and have a laugh,
Join in the fun, take a bubble bath.
For beneath the calm, joy leaps and bounds,
In the tranquil depths, laughter resounds.

Dreaming in Blue

In a realm where fish wear hats,
Jellybeans swim with mismatched spats.
Octopuses juggle shiny pearls,
While seahorses dance in twirling swirls.

Waves chuckle like a playful child,
Crabs do the cha-cha, unbeguiled.
Starfish throw parties on sandy floors,
With conch-shell speakers and clam-shell doors.

Turtles race in flashy speedos,
Blowing bubbles that transform to tantos.
Mermaids sing of romance gone wrong,
As dolphins harmonize with a silly song.

So dive into laughter, don't be shy,
For the ocean hides fun beneath the sky.
With each splash and giggle, let joy subdue,
In this whimsical world painted in blue.

Labyrinth of the Sea

Where seaweed's a maze and fish play tag,
Anemones wave like a multicolored rag.
Dolphins fly past with a wink and a flip,
While clams quietly plot the next big trip.

A big blue whale makes a silly face,
As clownfish whoop in a fuzzy embrace.
Sardines in sync perform a ballet,
While turtles take selfies and swim away.

The electric eel gives hair-raising shocks,
While crabs roam about in mismatched socks.
Anglerfish giggle beneath their bright lure,
In the labyrinth where fun is the cure.

With treasure chests filled with bubblegum treats,
Merfolk sharing jokes, bringing comical feats.
So swim through the whims, let your laughter flow,
In this underwater realm, let your joy overflow.

The Abyss Beckons

In shadows deep where whispers play,
A squid wears glasses, claims he's smart every day.
A grouper's telling jokes as he puffs out his chest,
While angelfish giggle, "Who's the silliest guest?"

Bubbles pop like popcorn, with laughter around,
As deep-sea creatures frolic, joy full and profound.
A pufferfish dons a party hat wide,
Waving hello to the ocean's slippery slide.

Ships lurk above, but who cares if they see?
As long as there's fun, it's a wild jubilee!
The shadows may whisper, but hear this cackle,
The abyss is alive with its own merry tackle.

So heed the call of the deep and the vast,
Let go of your worries, forget the past.
Join the dancing eels and the giggling whales,
In an abyss that's bursting with vibrant tales.

Beneath Coral Canopies

Where coral grows like candy, oh so bright,
Clownfish wear bowties, it's quite the sight.
Bubble-blowing sea turtles laugh with glee,
As angelfish twirl in a grand jubilee.

The octopus opens a coffee shop,
With espresso served hot and pastries on top.
While dolphins practice their stand-up routine,
The sea cucumbers cheer, "This is a scene!"

Conch shells are trumpets, played in the breeze,
As sea stars tap dance with effortless ease.
Anemones giggle, swaying to beats,
While all of the fish flash their sparkly feats.

So dive in the currents, let your spirit soar,
For under the waves, laughter's never a bore.
In the coral cathedrals, where silliness reigns,
Let joy be the tide that never restrains.

Veiled Currents

Bubbles pop with giggles loud,
A fish in glasses, swimming proud.
Octopuses roll in silly dance,
While clams do join in a wobbly prance.

Seaweed whispers, 'What's the fuss?'
A crab in slippers, oh what a plus!
Jellyfish float with umbrellas wide,
As dolphins surf on a slick tide.

Depths Uncharted

Mermaids braid their jellyfish hair,
While sea turtles try to form a pair.
Starfish twirl, a disco ball,
Declaring, 'Come join our underwater hall!'

A shrimp plays hopscotch on the sand,
With a seahorse as a game's grandstand.
Anemones cheer, they wiggly sway,
In this goofy, oceanic play.

Lurking in the Blue

A whale with sunglasses strikes a pose,
And fishes gossip, pointed nose.
The squids crack jokes, their ink in flight,
As sea cucumbers giggle with delight.

Worms in tuxedos dash to the show,
Urchins bounce, they steal the glow.
Inside a clam, a party's hot,
With clam chowder trying to join the plot.

Ghosts of the Sea

Ghostly fish with sheets so white,
Float by, giving all a fright.
But they just want to sing and dance,
In their underwater, wiggly trance.

A pirate's parrot lost his way,
Chasing bubbles, it's lost today.
On seaweed swings, the phantoms play,
Spooking fish in a comical way.

Coral Labyrinth

In the coral maze, where fish do roam,
A clownfish lost, he thought it home.
Turning round and round, oh what a sight,
He bumped into an octopus, who laughed in delight.

A starfish waved, as he passed by,
'Don't get too lost, or you might just cry!'
To which the fish replied, 'No worries, mate,
This maze is way cooler than a plastic plate.'

They spun and swirled in colors so bright,
While seaweeds danced, in the shimmering light.
The octo grinned wide, ink swirling like ink,
'Next time, bring snacks, don't overthink!'

So through the coral, they made quite the scene,
A labyrinth of laughter, oh where have they been?
Among bubbles and giggles, and not one dull frown,
In their watery world, they wore the crown.

The Ocean's Veil

Behind the kelp, a secret resides,
A crab in disguise, oh how it hides.
In polka dots and stripes, he prances with flair,
'Catch me if you can!' he shouts from his lair.

A seahorse giggles, it's quite the parade,
'Your outfit, dear crab, should surely be spayed!'
But the crab just twirled, proud of his style,
'I'm the best-dressed crustacean, by a nautical mile!'

Whales hum a tune, could it be a joke?
While octopi whisper, and start to poke.
'This dress code is wild, but let's have some fun,
In our underwater rave, we're never outdone!'

So with flippers and fins, the party began,
An undersea dance, a bizarrely grand plan.
With laughter and bubbles, they swayed to the beat,
In the ocean's grand veil, life's pretty sweet.

Treasures of the Dark Waters

In the depths of the sea, treasure's a joke,
While pirates search for gold, a fish just pokes.
'You think gems are great? Look at my scales!
Shining and twinkling, I'm better than whales!'

A clam opens wide, revealing a shoe,
'Found this old thing, it still fits me too!'
As fish gather 'round, they burst into cheer,
'Who knew dark waters held fashion right here?'

A gnome lost his hat, a boot floats on by,
A warning sign reads, 'Danger! Don't try!'
While crabs make a throne out of forgotten things,
'We'll rule the deep sea, like underwater kings!'

So they danced with glee, under shadows so deep,
Treasures of the sea, making memories to keep.
With laughter their fortune, in the ocean so blue,
They found joy in the treasure, who knew that it's true?

Whispers of the Tide

The tide whispers softly, a joke to be told,
'Why did the fish refuse to be sold?'
He wiggled his tail, and filled up with pride,
'Because I'm too awesome to be a fish fry!'

A sea turtle laughed, flipping back in the wave,
'Friend, you're quite right, be bold and be brave!'
While dolphins squeaked tunes, a chorus so sweet,
'Join the sea party, let's move those large feet!'

The rocks echoed giggles, as barnacles joined,
'We're dancing too, don't leave us behind!'
With shells acting silly, and bubbles that pop,
The whispers grew louder, as laughter won't stop.

As sunset approached, they twirled in delight,
The tide carried tales into the night.
From seaweed to starfish, all voices combined,
In the whispering waves, true joy they did find.

Secrets of Forgotten Depths

In the depths, a clam sings loud,
Chasing fish from a passing crowd.
A crab in a hat, quite the sight,
Dances away in the soft moonlight.

A lobster lost at a dance class,
Keeps stepping on a jellyfish's ass.
Sea cucumbers roll their eyes,
While seahorses try to disguise.

A turtle with tales oh-so grand,
Winks at a starfish, gives a hand.
But no one knows what it's about,
All the sea critters just laugh and shout.

Echoes of giggles swirl and twirl,
Under the waves, watch the shells whirl.
Every splash tells a joke, my friend,
In the depths, laughter knows no end.

Lyrics from the Ocean's Floor

The octopus plays the ukulele,
While clams clap along, feeling snazzy.
A flounder acts as the hype man,
Throwing backbeats, oh yes, he can!

Jellyfish glow, doing the twist,
Entangled, yet they can't resist.
A school of fish forms a conga line,
Moving together, oh so divine.

Anemones groove with funky flair,
While a crab keeps fixing his hair.
An orca sings a high-pitched note,
As seaweed sways, they all emote.

Lyrics bubble up like sweet soda,
In the ocean's depths, it's quite the moda.
Every splash a note, every wave a rhyme,
An underwater concert, oh so sublime!

Lost Tales of the Sea

Once a dolphin named Silly Joe,
Tried to surf on a giant float.
He flipped and flopped, what a face,
The whale laughed hard, oh what grace!

A fish with dreams of being a star,
Wore sunglasses and a sparkly guitar.
But all his tunes were out of key,
And even the barnacles fled with glee.

A mermaid spins tales, oh so tall,
About how she once played basketball.
But everyone knows, much to her shame,
She missed the net—what a claim to fame!

In the depths, stories weave and twine,
Making each fishery a punchline.
Under the water, giggles ring free,
As laughter bubbles up from the sea.

Murky Horizons

A fish in a tux tips his hat,
Winks at a squid, 'What's up with that?'
They swim through the fog, making a scene,
As crabbing crabs play in between.

Clownfish chuckle, they're just too bright,
In murky waters, what a delight!
A puffer fish pops in surprise,
With a mouthful of seaweed chips, oh the prize!

A catfish with whiskers quite grand,
Holds a tea party on the sand.
All the sea critters come for the cake,
But the grouper sneezes, oh what a mistake!

In the depths of the blue, where shadows play,
Every fish tells a joke, every wave a sway.
So dive with a smile, let laughter arise,
In the murky horizons, joy never dies!

The Unseen Tide

Fish in tuxedos, swim in style,
Crabs playing cards, they laugh and smile.
The seaweed dances, a cheeky jig,
While octopuses compete with a wig.

A whale cracks jokes, it's quite absurd,
Telling tales of a lost purple bird.
Starfish play poker, always on hold,
Their secrets hidden, yet all unfold.

Turtles tell stories of the sand of yore,
While seahorses gossip about the shore.
Anemones giggle, a ticklish spree,
Underwater laughs, so wild and free.

The tide rolls in with laughter and cheer,
Bringing jests from creatures we rarely hear.
So if you splash down, take heed of this,
For the ocean hides tales that beguile with bliss.

Enigmas of the Nautical Realm

Clams wearing glasses, solving their clues,
Dolphins in bowties, sipping on brews.
An octopus artist paints with flair,
While guppies gossip without a care.

The eels are a band, strumming their tunes,
At midnight dances beneath crescent moons.
Pufferfish puff up and claim the stage,
Making all fish chuckle, quite the rage.

Crabs copy moves from the latest trend,
While sea cucumbers just pretend.
The jellyfish waltz, a graceful parade,
Beneath dazzling bubbles, their secrets laid.

Shells whisper tales that no one can hear,
Of treasure hunts and secrets so dear.
Every ripple and wave shows just a part,
Of the goofy fun hidden in ocean's heart.

Beneath the Warlike Sea

Sharks in armor, ready to spar,
With fishy comedies, they raise the bar.
Swordfish duel with a flick of their fins,
While clam-shells giggle at their silly sins.

Pirates search for gold, but can't find a thing,
The treasure they seek? Just a rubber ring!
Octopuses plot with their eight-armed might,
While seahorses snicker, it's quite a sight.

Barnacles grumble about the rent they owe,
To a crab landlord causing quite the show.
Starfish stick together through thick and thin,
Laughing at battles they never did win.

So sail away, matey, with a grin so wide,
For beneath those waves, there's fun to abide.
The warlike sea hides laughter and cheer,
In the depths of the ocean, it's all crystal clear!

Nautical Shadows

Bubbles of laughter escape a fish,
They swim through shadows, full of swish.
A school of minnows creates a charade,
Conducting a play in the glimmering shade.

Eels hiding giggles behind coral walls,
Tickle the sea urchins, laughter calls.
Urchins just roll, they can't quite react,
As laughter erupts in the deep sea act.

A dolphin tricks gulls, what a cunning plan,
While clowns of the sea joke like they can!
The sea cucumber sneezes, dislodging some sand,
Creating a mist that the sea critters planned.

Whispers of mirth in the ocean abound,
In shadows and currents where cheer can be found.
So hold your breath and dive down to see,
The funny side of life where fish roam free.

Ghosts of the Water's Edge

In the shallow surf they play,
Giggling fish in disarray.
A crab with shades, oh what a sight,
Dancing clams, under the moonlight.

A splash of joy, a finned parade,
Jellyfish juggling, not afraid.
With seaweed wigs and sandcastle dreams,
The ocean chuckles, or so it seems.

Bubbles rise like giggles loud,
A dolphin donned in a rainbow shroud.
They race through currents, laugh and glide,
Those ghostly spirits, full of pride.

Watch out for that seal with a hat,
Taking selfies, oh imagine that!
They'll haunt your stories, day and night,
These water ghosts, a comical fright.

Fables of the Deep Blue

Coral castles, tales of yore,
Where mermaids snore and sea turtles roar.
A lobster bard with a cracked old shell,
Tells stories where seaweed spirits dwell.

A fish in a bowtie spins a yarn,
About a frog with dreams to charm.
Tangled in laughter, they all convene,
In the shimmery lure of the ocean sheen.

Pirate squids with ink-red pens,
Write the tales of fishy friends.
While octopuses perform their plays,
In the glow of the moon's soft rays.

So gather 'round, let's share a cheer,
With guffaws echoing far and near.
In the deep blue, laughter flows,
In fables told, where joy just grows.

Whispers from the Deep

Listen closely, the sea has tricks,
With sea cucumbers, having their kicks.
A clam recounts its dull old tale,
While sea horses dance without fail.

Beware the whispers of cheeky eels,
They'll spin you stories that no one feels.
Sing along with a flatfish, so bright,
Underwater parties last all night.

The stingrays glide with humor's grace,
Pulling pranks in a swirling race.
Bubble trails mark where laughter flows,
Among the critters, anything goes!

So wrap yourself in seafoam's giggle,
Join the fun, let the currents wiggle.
Whispers float, both near and far,
In ocean depths, we all bizarre.

Secrets of the Abyss

Down in the gloom where shadows play,
A ticklish squid is on the way.
With jiggly winks and silly poses,
It tells of plants that sneeze like roses!

A shark in specs reads the news,
While puffers pounce in playful hues.
They argue over who's the best,
For laughter's their ultimate quest.

The octopus juggles with grand delight,
As tiny shrimp dance in sheer fright.
Secrets swim, but joy won't fade,
In the belly of the ocean, we parade.

So come, my friend, let's dive today,
In the secrets where fish love to play.
In depths where giddiness swirls and spins,
The abyss reveals a world of grins.

Whispers of the Deep

A fish in a tux, quite dapper you see,
Dances with squid, oh so whimsically.
Crabs wear top hats, they strut with such flair,
While dolphins juggle fish, it's a real underwater affair.

The octopus knits, with eight arms in a twist,
Making sweaters for turtles who can't resist.
Starfish tell jokes, but they're always so flat,
Making the sea cucumbers say, "What's up with that?"

Anemones wink, with their colorful frills,
As clams play the trumpet, giving folks thrills.
Waves giggle softly, tickling the shore,
While mermaids in laughter just want to explore.

Bubbles pop loudly, a tune that's so sweet,
As seahorses race, oh what a silly feat.
Underneath the foam, where all things are bright,
The ocean's a party, what a jovial sight!

Secrets of the Sunken Shore

A treasure chest opens, full of socks and gum,
What pirates call gold, must be a big bummer!
Sunken ships dance, their sails down and frayed,
While crabs play their fiddles, so musically laid.

Mermaids with cupcakes, they share quite the feast,
But watch where you swim; there's a clam that won't cease!
Oysters are grumpy, they grumble and groan,
While jellyfish float like they've got a throne.

Bubbles are gossip, they swirl all around,
Telling fish tales that just can't be found.
Barnacles giggle, they stick without care,
Saying, "What's life without a little salt in the air?"

The seagulls are pranksters, they dive and they swoop,
Stealing your snacks in a most sneaky loop.
With laughter and fun on this whimsical floor,
The secrets down here are never a bore!

Echoes from the Abyss

In the depths of the sea, where shadows do play,
A crab tells a joke that just blows you away.
Fish in a bubble, floating on high,
Laughing at squids who are too shy to fly.

The echoes resound with a chuckle or two,
As sea stars share secrets 'bout things they once knew.
A whale's got a pun; it's not big, but it's grand,
Tickling the seaweed, it's all very planned.

Electric eels zap, making jokes on the fly,
As sea turtles giggle and wish to comply.
Corals like gossip, they sway to the sound,
In this vast underwater realm, fun is profound.

With jokes and with laughter, the currents do swirl,
In this wacky deep ocean, life's quite the whirl.
Echoes of humor, they bounce off the reefs,
Beneath the blue waves, it's pure comic relief!

Shadows in the Tidal Pool

In a pool by the shore, a clam does a dance,
While a crab in a wig gives the crowd quite a chance.
Starfish in shades watch the world go by,
Trading their secrets with the cockles nearby.

Seashells are gossiping under the sun,
"Did you hear about that fish? It's quite the fun run!"
Water striders skate on a very tight line,
While seaweed floats along, feeling mighty divine.

Anemones chuckle, tickled by waves,
As minnows all gather, their antics to save.
The moon pulls the tides, giving shells a grand show,
While crabs in their costumes steal the whole glow.

At twilight they gather, shadows blend and sway,
In the tidal pools' magic, come watch them at play.
With laughter and joy, in the salty embrace,
The shadows of fun find a glimmering place!

Tales of the Veiled Depths

Bubbles rise and fish all laugh,
A crab's doing the goofy gaffe.
Octopuses juggle seashells neat,
While turtles dance on finny feet.

Seaweed's having a wild parade,
Starfish wearing shades, unafraid.
A dolphin sings a silly tune,
Rhythm echoing 'neath the moon.

Whales exchange their fishy jokes,
Clams giggle in their shell-bound coats.
Even pirates are caught off guard,
Their treasure's now a playful card!

From the depths where sea creatures cheer,
Life's a party, it's crystal clear.
So dive right in, join the fun,
In the ocean, there's room for everyone!

Calls from the Ocean's Heart

The tide plays tricks, a bubbling sound,
As mermaids giggle, spinning round.
Their hair a mess of seaweed strands,
Creating chaos with silly hands.

A fish in glasses reads the news,
Sands of time bring gossip views.
Anemones swaying to the beat,
Their waves dance lively, neat and sweet.

Crabs with hats march in a line,
While plankton twirl in soft divine.
Each current whispers tales of cheer,
That echo through the marin' sphere.

So listen close to bubbling calls,
Of fishy tales in ocean halls.
With chuckles rolling, waves collide,
Adventure waits beneath the tide!

Enigmatic Currents

In swirling waters, jokes arise,
A squirt of ink, a great surprise!
Electric eels zap the floor,
While fishy friends shout out for more.

An ocean's game of hide and seek,
With seahorses playing hide-and-peek.
The grouchy grouper grumbles low,
But a ticklish octopus steals the show.

Every wave a laugh to share,
A kraken's dance, how rare, how fair!
The tides pull pranks on passing boats,
While dolphins giggle, sharing notes.

Each flick and splash brings stories bright,
Of sea-salted shenanigans in flight.
So dive together, have a laugh,
In the ocean's depths, take a gaff!

Submerged Sorrows

Not sorrows here, just bubbles and cheer,
Sharks play tag—oh what a year!
A turtle in a fancy hat,
Looks quite posh in a hula mat.

Flounders flounder in their own way,
Trying to catch the plankton ballet.
A sea cucumber's got the moves,
With squishy grooves that just improve.

Blowfish puff up, a sight to see,
While little shrimp burst out in glee.
An old sunken chest holds jokes so bright,
Tickling the fish with sheer delight.

So leave your woes upon the shore,
In these depths, there's always more.
Laughter reigns in the waves around,
As underwater giggles resound!

Winds Beneath the Waves

Bubbles rise and fish do dance,
A sea cucumber wears pants!
Octopus tries to spin a tune,
But passes gas like a balloon.

Mollusks giggle, dolphins play,
A crab shimmies in dismay.
With every splash, a riddle grows,
Who stole my shoes? Nobody knows!

A jellyfish in a top hat winks,
Swirling around, it hilariously sinks.
Parrots squawk, a whale joins in,
Let's all dance, with a splashy grin!

Beneath the waves, where secrets sway,
Creatures jest and prance all day.
When the tide rolls in with a goofy grin,
You can bet the fish will win!

Hidden Depths

A clam told a joke, but no one laughed,
Puffers puffed up, the humor half-calfed.
A starfish joked, "I'm looking to shine!"
The seaweed waved like a drunken vine.

Sardines all huddled, telling tall tales,
Of swimming so fast they could outrun gales.
Seahorses giggled in matching attire,
Tail-to-tail, they formed a choir.

A turtleneck turtle gave fashion advice,
"Wear your shell proudly, it's quite precise!"
And as they swayed with a splash and a bob,
Everyone knew they had a great job.

In depths obscure where laughter flows,
Giggling fish bring forth their prose.
When waves crash down with a joyful cheer,
The ocean's secrets are fun and clear!

The Aquatic Riddle

Why did the fish cross the sea?
To show off its new GPS, you see!
A turtle typing on a tiny phone,
Said, "I'll tweet my swim, I'm not alone!"

Anemones laughed, all wriggly and spry,
"Tangled in weeds? Oh me, oh my!"
A grouper grinned, with a big, flashy sure,
"I'm here for the laughs, not the lure!"

They held a contest, the Nautilus judged,
With frantic laughter, the crowd was nudged.
A joke about krill, oh what a sight,
Fish in the background, giggling with delight!

In this realm, where silliness swims,
Lighthearted jests are sure to brim.
Beneath the surface, where tides play tricks,
Funny tales echo like slippery kicks!

Cryptic Currents

Current flows, but what's the catch?
Crabs in tuxedos ready to hatch!
A dolphin sneezes, bubbles galore,
"Excuse me," it says, "I just swam from shore!"

A fish in a hat, thinking it grand,
"Tell me, my friend, is this seaweed tanned?"
The lobsters chuckled, tail-twitching fast,
Each joke a wave that forever will last.

Eels tangled up in a game of charades,
Playing hide-and-seek with oceanic shades.
The currents giggle, they swirl and glide,
As laughter dances on the smelly tide.

A kraken pranks with a playful grip,
"My tentacles tickle—come take a dip!"
In waters deep where fun is rife,
Secrets of laughter bring fish to life!

Legends of the Sea's Embrace

A curious crab wore a hat,
While gossiping with a sleepy cat.
They debated the taste of jellyfish stew,
And wondered if mermaids liked it too.

A fish with a mustache danced with flair,
Spinning tales of treasure beyond compare.
But every time he spun round and round,
He got dizzy, and fell to the ground.

A wise old octopus took a nap,
Dreaming of launching a sea-faring map.
When he awoke, with ink in a plume,
He drew a route to a giant sea broom.

They laughed and they squealed, oh what a show,
With splashes of bubbles to brighten the flow.
For legends are silly in ocean's expanse,
Where even the barnacles want to dance.

Dances of the Forgotten Fathoms

A starfish tried to boogie with flair,
But lost both his legs and sat in despair.
A rogue little sprat said, "Join in my song!"
While the seaweed swayed, it all felt so wrong.

Crabs hosted parties with snacks galore,
Eating popcorn that washed up on shore.
But the seagulls swooped in with a cheeky squawk,
Stealing their snacks for a beachside walk.

Whale songs echoed from deep in the blue,
Telling tales of the time they lost a shoe.
A dolphin just giggled, gave a wink and grin,
"Don't worry, dear friend, we'll find it again!"

Together they twirled in delightful dismay,
In the dance hall of bubbles, all had their say.
With laughter as loud as the waves did crash,
The fathoms held secrets that swirled in a flash.

Silence of the Hidden Reefs

In the quiet deep, a lobster did chirp,
"No one hears me, I'm great at the burp!"
But a clownfish giggled at his grand jest,
"Is laughter an echo or just your best?"

A shy little seahorse munched on some grass,
While pondering why fish never wear class.
He concocted a tale of fins so divine,
And dressed all his friends for a ball so fine.

Then a group of bright urchins, sharp yet polite,
Said, "We'd win a dance-off, if it's at night!"
But their spiky attire caused some dismay,
So they rolled in the sand and let worries stray.

As laughter arose from coral so deep,
Nemo and friends vowed, "This secret we'll keep!"
The silence was golden, yet giggles would swell,
In the hidden reefs where the fish liked to dwell.

Veils of Mist and Salt

A mermaid forgot where she parked her shell,
As the slap of the waves sang her sweet farewell.
With sea cucumbers giggling, they locked arms tight,
"We'll help you find it, oh what a sight!"

The mist rolled in, it was thick as a stew,
A squid gave directions, all out of the blue.
"Take a left at the rock that looks like a shoe,
Then a right by the barnacle, the one that's brand new!"

They swam past a shark who was counting his gold,
"Call it a day, I'm getting too old!"
But the chase was on, with giggles and glee,
As they swirled through the sea like birds chasing spree.

Finally, they found her lost mode of transport,
Hiding in kelp, much to her export.
With a wave and a laugh, they said, "What a ball!"
In the veils of mist, they revelled for all.

Beneath the Salty Surface

A crab in a tux, quite dapper and proud,
Stomps on a starfish, much to the crowd.
They dance on the sand, in a ridiculous show,
With seaweed as bowties, stealing the show.

A dolphin named Ned wears shades like a pro,
Claims he can surf, but he's just too slow.
The fish all applaud, with bubbles in cheer,
As Ned takes a tumble, they laugh and they jeer.

An octopus juggles, with eight nimble hands,
He slips with his shellfish, they're scattered like bands.
The clams make a fuss, while the shrimp start to sing,
With a party so wild, they're inviting a fling.

So joyfully silly, this world down below,
Where creatures do antics and put on a show.
They laugh at their blunders; life's such a game,
In the salty surf, nothing's ever the same.

Hidden Treasures of Neptune

A treasure chest opens, but what's inside?
Just rubber chickens—oh, Neptune's pride!
Fish wear party hats, with confetti galore,
They throw a grand shindig on the ocean floor.

Mermaids in sequins, they sidestep and twirl,
Flipping their fins in a whimsical whirl.
A crab procures snacks; he thinks he's so sly,
But he's nibbling the hats as they flutter on by.

With a parrotfish yelling, 'I found gold for sale!'
Turns out it's a snail on a shiny old trail.
Turtles in sunglasses just lounge in the sand,
And sea cucumbers do their best on demand.

Oh, the artifacts gleam, but what's truly grand,
Are the laughter and joy that keeps growing unplanned.
Underneath all that water, where silliness dwells,
It's treasures of laughter that ring like sweet bells.

Riddles of the Ocean Floor

A fish named Fred asks, 'Where's my left fin?'
While his buddy Larry is stuck in a spin.
They go for a swim, but it's all quite absurd,
With a shark in a wig who claims he's a bird.

Coral reefs giggle, tickled by the brine,
As eels tell their stories with punchlines divine.
Anemones giggle, all swaying in time,
To sea shanties sung with a splashy rhyme.

A pirate squid hunts for a treasure chest,
But finds only bubbles and an old, squeaky vest.
He shrugs with a grin, 'Life's an ocean of fun!'
While chasing a seahorse that's on the run.

To dive or not dive? That's the big question,
While jellyfish wiggle with pure satisfaction.
In this watery world, jokes float like the seas,
Where laughter is constant, and everyone's pleased!

Echoing Secrets in the Brine

A seaweed detective, with a hat made of kelp,
Inquires with sly smiles, played out with a yelp.
Whispers and giggles drift through the blue,
As a clam gives a wink, and the stories ensue.

Why did the fish blush? 'I saw a sea star!'
Shellfish explode with hearty guffaws from afar.
The tides laugh along, echoing their cheer,
As playful finned dancers shake their fins near.

A whale sings a tune that tickles the heart,
While dolphins flip high, in this silly art.
With bubbles and giggles, they fill up the sea,
Making waves of laughter, just wild and free.

As kelp whispers secrets, without any care,
All creatures unite for a round of good fare.
In oceans so deep, with joy that entwines,
The echoes of laughter resound in the brine.

The Depth of Secrets

In the ocean's goofy grin,
Fish wear hats, all the way in.
Octopus plays chess with a shark,
While jellyfish glow in the dark.

Sea turtles laugh on a beach ball,
A clam shouts, 'Catch the last call!'
Starfish twirl like they own the floor,
While crabs dance out the ocean's door.

In conch shells, gossip flows free,
"Did you see what she wore? Oh me!"
Seahorses strut in their best attire,
Making waves with their funky choir.

Bubbles float up with a sigh,
As dolphins giggle, oh my, oh my!
Scratch your head, it's quite a scene,
Under the waves, it's silly and keen.

Enchanted Waters

Down below where the fish all smirk,
A mermaid sneezes, 'What a perk!'
With a splash and a giggle from a whale,
It's a fishy party at the bottom of the pale.

Eels slide by with a wink and a nod,
'We're all friends here, it's not so odd!'
Seashells whisper secrets of old,
While crabs tell tales that are ever so bold.

A school of fish dances in lines,
While sea urchins sip on the best brines.
The water's alive with laughter and cheer,
While a big old octopus drinks root beer!

Turtles breakdance on the sandy floor,
As waves keep rolling, begging for more.
In this enchantment, life takes a spin,
In the deep blue, where mischief begins!

Legends from the Deep

Oh, listen closely to fishy tales,
Of pirate gold and big, floppy sails.
A narwhal lost his silly hat,
He danced with sharks and a big old rat!

A whale took a dive, and oh what a sight,
Spitting water high, laughter took flight.
Fishes in tuxedos, they twirled and spun,
While seaweed waved like it's having fun.

Kraken's just misunderstood, you see,
Trying to play, not causing a spree.
With big, floppy arms, he just wants to hug,
But sailors scream, thinking he's a bug!

So here's to legends that teeter and sway,
In the comic depths where the sea-life play.
These stories will curl your toes with glee,
For the ocean's a stage, come join the spree!

Beneath the Sail

At dawn, where sailors haul their fish,
A catfish claims it's his only wish.
An octopus hitchhikes on a boat,
While seagulls chime in like they're on a float.

The captain laughs, 'Who's steering now?'
As a crab steals snacks — we'll take a bow!
Squid juggling with ink makes quite a mess,
While starfish cheer, 'We're the best, no less!'

Waves crash loud with a silly splash,
As dolphins leap like they're in a mash.
The sailboat sways to a rhythm so neat,
As fish swim by, tapping their feet.

And thus the stories carried by tide,
Of laughter and pranks that the ocean provides.
So join the fun beneath the sky,
Where fish tell tales that'll make you cry!

Shadows in the Current

There's a fish with a bowtie,
He dances and spins, oh my!
A crab with a monocle too,
Sipping tea in the deep blue.

An octopus plays the drums,
While the shrimp all cheer and hums.
They throw a bash without a care,
In the seaweed room of a fancy lair.

A whale wears a party hat,
Telling jokes, imagine that!
With sea cucumbers in tow,
They laugh at the underwater show.

The eels twirl and slide,
In their elegant slippery stride.
As the bubbles rise and poke,
They giggle at every joke they've spoke.

Enigma of the Ocean Floor

A treasure chest full of socks,
With pearls and shiny rocks!
What were pirates really after?
Just old shoes, it's quite the laughter!

A sea turtle wears a crown,
Crowned with kelp, he strolls around.
He thinks he's the king of the deep,
But just snores while fishy friends peep.

Crabs in suits with big dreams,
Planning their big jelly-bean schemes.
They hold a meeting at the reef,
On how to win the prankster's chief.

With starfish clapping their arms,
And jellyfish sharing their charms,
They ride the waves with goofy flair,
Making bubbles in seaweed hair.

Beneath the Surface

Down where the sun doesn't reach,
A clownfish starts a speech.
'Why did the coral blush so bright?'
'It saw the ocean's funny sight!'

Anemones holding a play,
With sea horses leading the way.
They bow to the audience of shrimp,
As the seaweed sets the stage to limp.

A dolphin wears a silly wig,
Sinks to the bottom, does a jig.
With all the fish getting in line,
For a selfie with Mr. Grin Divine.

Seahorses giggle and chase,
Love to hang around for a race.
With sea cucumbers on a slide,
They splash and laugh at the tide.

Echoes of the Tides

In a cove where echoes sing,
A fish with a hat, quite the thing.
He tells tales of the great big sea,
With a wink and a wink, oh so free!

An urchin hosting a game show,
'Who wants to find the lost treasure glow?'
With contestants like crabs and snails,
All giggling at their funny fails.

A squid juggles shells on a whim,
While clownfish laugh on a limb.
The tide plays music so sweet,
As the underwater crowd takes a seat.

With bubbles popping like balloons,
They swim in tune to silly tunes.
For beneath it all, they know this fact,
The ocean's joy is a tangible act!

Whirls of Oceanic Wonder

A fish in a tux, what a sight to see,
Dancing with crabs, oh so fancy and free.
They twirl and they spin, with great grand flair,
Who knew sea life had such stylish hair?

A squid lost its shoe, it's flopping around,
While octopuses giggle, they've lost what they've found.
Sea turtles sigh, they're stuck in a race,
Judges nodding, it's a hilarious chase!

Whales pass a note, 'You've got great new moves!'
Dolphins are laughing, they're all in their grooves.
The coral is clapping, the clams cheer "Hooray!"
Even the plankton join in the play!

Oh, what a party beneath the big tides,
Where laughter and bubbles are great ocean rides!
Who knew the sea harbored such circus delight?
With every splash, there's new giggles in sight!

Depths Unknown

What's lurking down there? A blender, perhaps?
Or just Mr. Lobster looking for jabs?
Anemones giggle, they wave their long hands,
Tickling the fish, oh ain't it just grand?

Eels wear their ties with a casual air,
Snapping their selfies, they don't have a care.
The sunken ships sing a calypso of old,
Fishes wear sunglasses, feeling quite bold.

Crabs hold a meeting, their shells polished bright,
Arguing loudly about who's left the light.
A conch blows the horn, oh what a fun start,
As clams do a dance, all with rhythmic heart.

Bubbles are bursting, they make quite the sound,
Fish laughing loudly, 'Oh, don't lose your crown!'
In depths yet unknown, they wear silly smiles,
Creating a grotto with laughter in piles!

Beneath the Blue Expanse

A sea cucumber moans, 'What's the latest news?'
While seahorses gossip, wearing bright blues.
Starfish are lounging, socks mismatched in style,
Finding their rhythm, they dance with a smile.

The jellyfish bounce in their gooey parade,
With rhythms so funky, you'd think they were made!
Orange fish shuffle, ooh-ing with glee,
'When's our next beach day? Let's all suntan free!'

Pufferfish puff, oh what a round sight,
Trying to squeeze through a door way too tight.
A sea turtle yawns, 'Just a moment to rest,'
But laughter erupts, for he's giggling the best.

With bubbles and bubbles, they're spinning around,
Kooky sea creatures, lost but then found.
Beneath the blue stretch, where silliness flows,
In this vibrant world, anything goes!

Secrets Entwined in Seaweed

A pirate's old treasure? Just seaweed and twine,
With starfish deciding the best way to dine.
"Let's make a salad with bits that we find!"
The clams open wide, and laughter's unconfined.

The crabs in their jackets, a fashion parade,
Strutting so boldly, like they're on a crusade.
"We'll show them our moves!" one excitedly said,
As fish joined in, swirling their tails overhead.

The secrets of seaweed, they draw you in close,
Like a ticklish tickle from an overgrown ghost.
Eels sharing stories of their wild dreams,
While undersea laughter flows like silver streams.

The ocean's a stage, where silliness flows,
A mismatch of life and giggles in throes.
Beneath green fronds, where the playtime is sweet,
Seaweed wraps secrets, so funny and neat!

www.ingramcontent.com/pod-product-compliance
Lightning Source LLC
Chambersburg PA
CBHW060145230426
43661CB00003B/570